THE STORY OF
LIFE ON EARTH

For Edward

OXFORD
UNIVERSITY PRESS

Great Clarendon Street, Oxford OX2 6DP

Oxford University Press is a department of the University of Oxford.
It furthers the University's objective of excellence in research, scholarship, and education
by publishing worldwide in

Oxford New York

Athens Auckland Bangkok Bogotá Buenos Aires Calcutta
Cape Town Chennai Dar es Salaam Delhi Florence Hong Kong Istanbul
Karachi Kuala Lumpur Madrid Melbourne Mexico City Mumbai
Nairobi Paris São Paulo Singapore Taipei Tokyo Toronto Warsaw

with associated companies in Berlin Ibadan

Oxford is a registered trade mark of Oxford University Press
in the UK and in certain other countries

Created and produced by Nicholas Harris, Joanna Turner
and Claire Aston, Orpheus Books Ltd

Illustrated by Nicki Palin

Scientific consultant: Professor Michael Benton,
Department of Geology, University of Bristol

Copyright © 1999 Orpheus Books Ltd

First published 1999

British Library Cataloguing in Publication Data available.

Hardback ISBN 0-19-910579-0
Paperback ISBN 0-19-910580-4

1 3 5 7 9 10 8 6 4 2

Printed in Belgium

THE STORY OF
LIFE ON EARTH

Written by
NICHOLAS HARRIS

Illustrated by
NICKI PALIN

OXFORD
UNIVERSITY PRESS

Millions and millions and millions of years ago ... nothing lived in our world.

There were no people or animals.
No trees or grass.
There wasn't even a fish in the sea.

The land was just rock.
Nothing could grow.

The only sounds were the waves crashing on the
seashore and the wind howling.
Nothing was alive.

Then, millions and millions and millions of years later …

... something stirred at the bottom of the sea.

Tiny jellyfish drifted in the water, and worms wriggled through the mud.

One by one, other strange creatures appeared.
Some had lots of legs and scuttled along the sea bed.

Some had spikes and crept slowly about.

One had five mushroom-shaped eyes on its head, and teeth on the end of an arm.

One looked a bit like a fish, but didn't have any fins.

Millions and millions and millions of years later ...

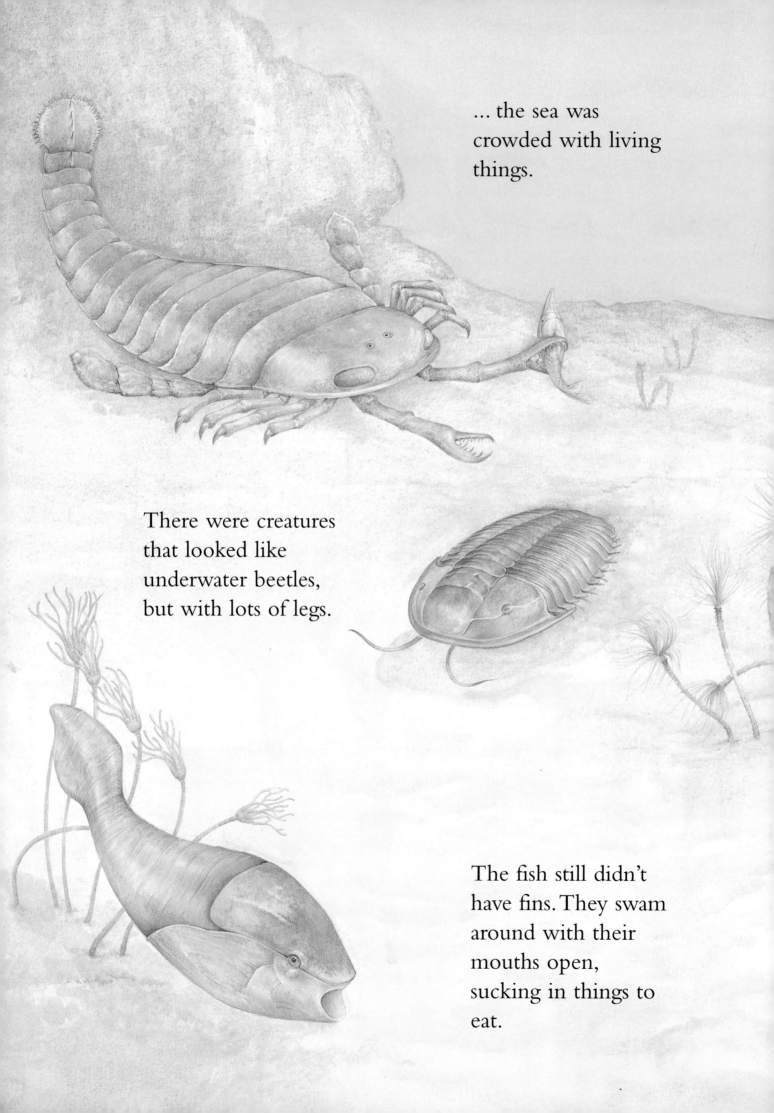

... the sea was crowded with living things.

There were creatures that looked like underwater beetles, but with lots of legs.

The fish still didn't have fins. They swam around with their mouths open, sucking in things to eat.

Later, some fish did grow fins. They also grew huge jaws with fearsome teeth, and went chasing after smaller creatures.

Millions and millions of years later ...

... things started to happen on land.

Plants burst through the mud close to the water's edge,
then spread further and further inland.
The rocky land became green and alive.

Insects and creepy-crawly creatures fed on the plants.
Some of the fish that swam in the lakes and streams
began to feed on them.

The fish would dash out of the water to grab the
biggest, juiciest insects.

The fishes' fins became strong and plump, and they used
them like legs.
They could walk about on land and breathe fresh air.

Millions and millions of years later ...

... some fish found they could live on land nearly all the time.
Their fins grew toes to help them walk better, and their flat, fishy tails changed to long, straight ones.
Now they only went back to the water to lay their eggs, and to cool off in the heat.

Meanwhile, some plants had started to grow tall and straight.
They were the first trees.

The climate became hot and rainy, and before long, there were thick, dark forests everywhere.

Huge dragonflies buzzed and flitted through the new forests.
Long wormy creatures scuttled about on their many legs.

The fish-with-legs wallowed about in the dank, dark, muddy ponds, grunting and snorting.

Meanwhile, some little animals darted through the high trees.

They had long, smooth bodies like the fish-with-legs, but they looked more like lizards.

They had learnt to lay their eggs on land, so they no longer had to spend any time in the water at all.

They were the first reptiles.

Then, millions and millions of years later ...

... the dense forest had disappeared.
It was still very hot on the land, but now it was much
drier.

Some of the bigger reptiles lay around in the sunshine.
Great sails of skin rose from their backs.

Millions and millions of years later ...

... there were many different sorts of reptile.

Some had stout,
bony bodies and
spiky heads.

Some had tusks
and snuffled
about like pigs.

Some had long
legs and could
run quite fast.

Some were quite
small and grew
furry coats.

The long-legged reptiles began to move about on
their two back legs.
They found that they could run even faster this way.
They had long tails to help them keep their balance.
Their arms were short and strong, good for grabbing
things to eat.

They were the first dinosaurs.

The dinosaurs ruled the world for millions of years, and came in all shapes and sizes.

Some were enormous.
Their long necks and tails were so long that they were easily the biggest, longest creatures ever to walk on this earth.

Other dinosaurs were as small as cats.

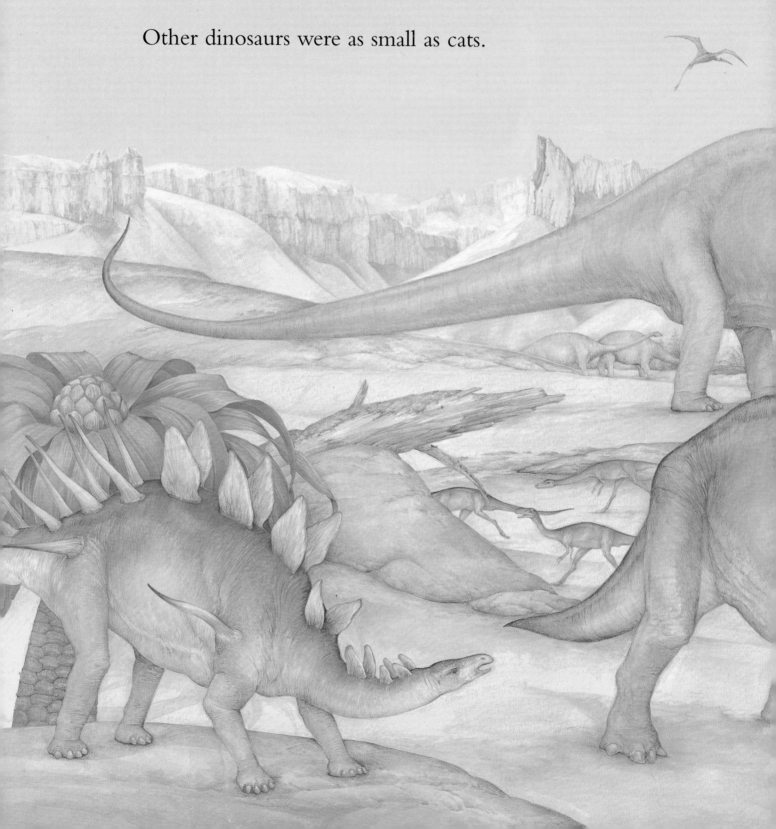

Some dinosaurs, like Diplodocus, were gentle creatures, content to munch leaves all day.
Others, like Tyrannosaurus rex, were fierce and dangerous.
They were as tall as houses, and could run as fast as a car.
Their teeth were as long and sharp as daggers.

Many dinosaurs had built-in weapons, such as spikes on their backs, horns on their heads, or clubs at the tips of their tails.

The little furry creatures hid themselves away, and only dared to come out at night while the dinosaurs were sleeping.

They were the first mammals.

Some tiny, light dinosaurs grew feathers, and found that they could glide from tree to tree.

They were the first birds.

Other reptiles flew in the sky with the birds.
They had wings made of skin, and large heads with long, powerful beaks.
Some of these flying reptiles grew to the size of small aeroplanes.

There were also reptiles still living in the sea.
Some of them looked like fish, with fins and tails to help them to swim fast.
Others had long, snaky necks.

Then, quite suddenly, all of the dinosaurs vanished from the face of the Earth.
No one knows exactly why.

Perhaps a huge rock from outer space crashed into our planet.
The dust and smoke from the explosion may have plunged the world into darkness for years on end.
Maybe it became too cold for the dinosaurs.

Whatever happened, it meant that, at last, the mammals could come out of hiding.

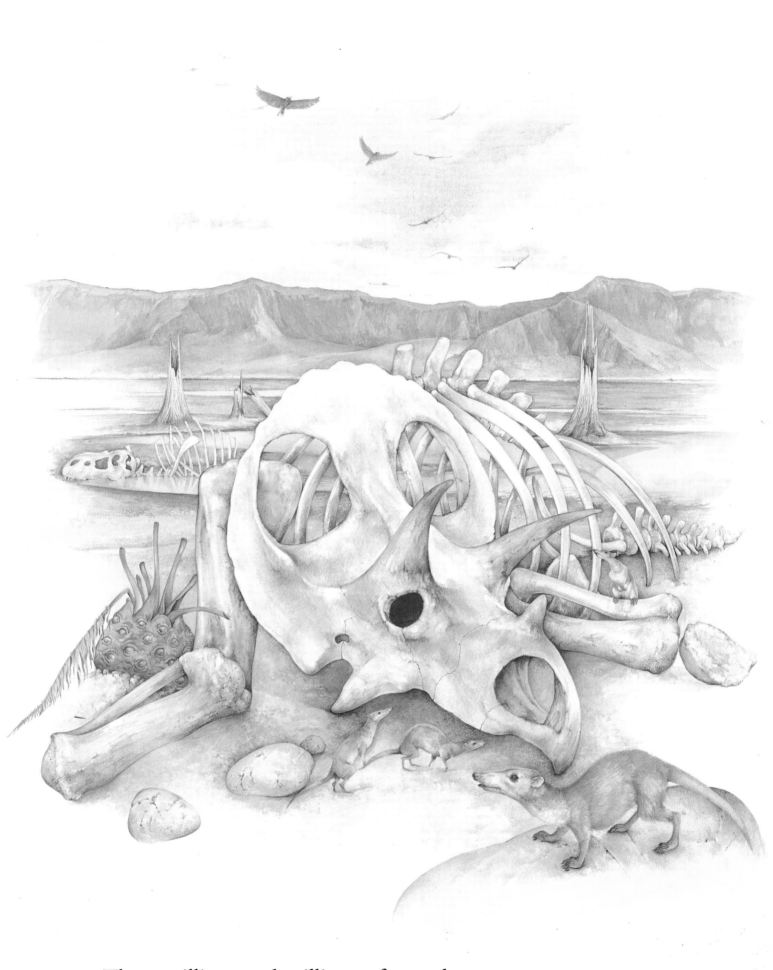

Then, millions and millions of years later ...

... there were many different sorts of mammal.

Some of them looked quite like animals alive today.

There were elephants with tusks that pointed backwards instead of forwards.
There were giraffes with short necks.

There were horses the size of cats.
There were guinea pigs the size of hippos.

Birds sang in the trees.
Insects hovered over flowers.

But there were still no people.

And then, millions of years later ...

... the ice came.

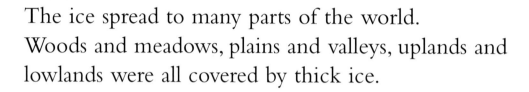

The ice spread to many parts of the world.
Woods and meadows, plains and valleys, uplands and
lowlands were all covered by thick ice.

Animals could only live in places that the ice didn't
reach.
It was very cold and wintry all year round.

The woolly
rhinoceros had a
thick, furry coat to
keep it warm.

The cave bear
escaped the worst of
the weather by
sleeping all through
the winter.

The mammoth was the mightiest creature in the ice kingdom.

But although its woolly coat kept it safe from the ice, it wasn't safe from a mammal that hunted it with sharp spears.

Humans had arrived.

At first, people had to go looking for food in the wild, just like all the other animals.
They hunted, fished, and found nuts and berries in the forest.
They lived in caves or in tents made from branches and animal skins.

Then the people discovered how to grow plants which they could use for food.
They also tamed wild animals and kept them.

Now people didn't have to wander in search of things to eat.
They could build villages and live there all the time.

Thousands of years passed.

There were more and more people, living in more and more villages.

People cut down trees to make room for their crops and their animals.
They hunted animals and caught fish.

Some of the villages grew into towns, then large cities.

People built railways, roads, bridges, and airports.
They dug large holes in the ground.

People needed more and more space.

Animals that live in the wild need space, too.
But people usually get their way, so many animals have lost their homes.

Millions and millions of years ago, nothing lived in our world.
Millions and millions of years later, the dinosaurs ruled.
And millions and millions of years later, humans arrived.

Millions of years from now, who will continue the story of life on Earth?